MW00389765

This Book is the Property of

_____

One Line a Day: Five Year Memory Book (Journal Diary)

FastForwardPublishing.com

ISBN-13: 978-1519408990
ISBN-10: 1519408994

TABLE OF CONTENTS

      Do I have to start on January 1st?
      What do I write about?
      How do I keep from being overwhelmed by a 5-year
      commitment?
      What if I'm inspired to write more than one line?
      Why don't I just do this online?

WHAT IS A 5-YEAR ONE LINE A DAY JOURNAL?

It's a quick, easy and fun way to track the ups and downs of your life. There are 365 pages (each representing a day of the year) with space for five entries for each day (one for each of 5 years) so you can revisit previous thoughts and memories over 5 years as you return to each page to write about the current day.

January 2

2014 Rainy and cold all day - missing summer - need sun. Both kids came home early from school complaining of sore throats, taking them to doctor tomorrow am.

2015 It took 45 minutes today for the usual 20 minute commute home from work; thank goodness I had the "In the Unlikely Event" audio book with me ... great book ... will recommend for neighborhood book club.

2016 Worried about mom's doctor appointment next week; she's getting forgetful and I can't stop thinking about Alzheimer's

2017 Got a call out of the blue from Bob North (6th grade homeroom); haven't heard from him in years; he'll be in town next Tuesday; we're having lunch.

2018 getting excited about vacation next week, but nervous about the plane ride

11

INTRODUCTION
by James Allen Proctor

Although keeping a journal seemed like a great idea, I never really got the hang of it.

Many times, I'd start one with great anticipation of, years in the future, looking back and remembering the details of what I was doing and thinking in the past. It never worked out. I'd start out strong and then neglect to update it for days, weeks or even months. Then, I'd get motivated to start up again, but the blank pages would make me feel like I needed to go back and fill in all the details from the time that had elapsed. This would turn into a marathon "catch up" journal entry that would make me feel like that journaling was an exhausting chore and fill me with excuses to quit. So, I'd put it on hold and forget about it.

But a year or two later, again thinking about how great it would be, years in the future, to have the ability to look back and remember the details of what I was doing and thinking in the past, I'd start another journal.

After abandoning many journals over the years, I learned about the concept of one line a day journals in which you only write one line per day. Whether it was a busy and exciting day or a boring and ordinary day, you just write one line. You're not creating a detailed account of your life, you're just jotting down a reminder of what was going on in your life at that particular point in time. And it only takes a minute or two at the end of the day. If you miss a day or two, it's no big deal to catch up.

For me, the one line a day journal is the answer, because it does not create a daunting task of writing in volume and it does not demand too much time. And, once I'd been jotting quick entries for a year, it started paying off in the way that originally attracted me to journaling. This year's entry is written below last year's entry which is written under the entry from the year before ... you see parallels and differences from year to year. It's very cool.

Best of all, instead of creating a stack of journals that you rarely (if ever) go back to peruse, you get a quick look at "same time/last year" that can bring back a flood of memories and thoughts. As a parent, it's a wonderful reminder of milestones (first holidays, first words, first day of school, etc.) -- which you probably have in a baby book somewhere that you never look at – and it's fun to see similarities and changes from year to year (mmm, my youngest kid always gets sick the first week of October). That being said, you don't need children to make this work, whether you are on your own, or living with a family (big or small) it can be incredibly interesting to be reminded of what you were doing and thinking a year (and years) ago today.

My take-away: A one line a day journal is a quick, easy and manageable way of journaling that pays off in a fun way that is worth far more than the effort expended. I hope you feel the same way.

James Allen Proctor

James Allen Proctor is a best-selling author who is known in the journaling world as the author of a popular series of Gratitude Journals including: *The Gratitude Journal* and *The 5-Minute Gratitude Journal*

HOW TO KEEP A ONE LINE A DAY JOURNAL

1. Go to today's date in your journal

2. Write in the current year in the next available entry (there's a space provided).

3. Write one line about today. What to write about? See the Frequently Asked Questions section of this book (page 7).

That's it. All it takes a couple of minutes a day and the special part is that you record your one daily line in the same spot for five years, so where you wrote your June 27, 2015 line is on the same page you write your June 27, 2016 line and June 27, 2017 line and so on. Each year you get to see what you wrote the previous year(s).

FREQUENTLY ASKED QUESTIONS

Do I have to start on January 1st?

No. You can start any day of the year. The key thing is to get started. The day your journal comes into your home whether it's May 13, January 1 or October 29 make your first entry, and then spend a couple of minutes every day. It's an easy habit to get into and it really starts paying off after you've been doing it a year and you can start comparing this day this year to this day last year (and previous years).

NOTE: You'll see that this journal has a day for February 29th, you'll only need that page once every 4 years (leap year).

What do I write about?

Try to capture the key moments or overall feel of your day in a phrase or two. Did you do something special? Did a family member do something interesting? How are you feeling physically? Mentally? Did something happen that made you happy, sad, annoyed, frustrated, silly, worried, excited, depressed, cheerful, etc.?

Don't try to describe everything that happened during the day, just one or two key moments/feelings, for example: "getting excited about vacation next week but nervous about the plane ride" or "Both kids came home early from school complaining of sore throats, taking them to doctor tomorrow am" or "Got a call out of the blue from Bob North (6th grade homeroom); haven't heard from him in years; he'll be in town next Tuesday; we're having lunch."

Don't worry about "boring" days because they're normal and capturing normalcy is fun as well. Entries like "Fell asleep on the couch watching 'Game of Thrones'" or "Came home exhausted, ate leftover lasagna for dinner; didn't even bother to re-heat it. Tasted good with a glass of red wine" or "It took 45 minutes today for the usual 20 commute home from work; thank goodness I had the 'In the Unlikely Event' audio book with me."

As well as activities, you can also write how you are feeling: "Worried about mom's doctor appointment next week; she's getting forgetful and I can't stop thinking about Alzheimer's" or "My first date with Jim is Friday. We're going to dinner at La Ciccia, very excited. Hoping it goes well."

If it is easier, you can always come up with "prompts" to help you with an entry.

Here are some examples:

What made today unusual?
What's the hardest thing I am dealing with right now?
What is my favorite current web site?

What was the weather today? Did this impact my plans or my mood?

What's the last thing I wanted but didn't get?

What were the kids up to today? Spouse? Significant other? Best friend?

Who last called me on the phone?

What made me laugh today?

What's the last thing I apologized for?

What did I buy today?

What annoyed me today?

What's my favorite TV show right now?

What did I have for dinner today?

What was the most expensive bill I paid last month?

If I had a super power, what would it be? Why?

What was my biggest accomplishment today? This week? This month?

In whose life did I make a difference today? How?

What book am I reading right now? Would you recommend it?

How is my health today on a scale of 1 to 10?

Who is the last person to tell me that they loved me?

What person do I wish I didn't have to deal with today?

How do I keep from being overwhelmed by a 5-year commitment?

Don't think of this as a big five year project. Think of it as something small you're going to do today. Don't think ahead. Take it one day at a time. It's like brushing your teeth before you go to bed: it's just two minutes every night; you don't think of it as of brushing your teeth for 60 hours (2 minutes per night x 365 nights x 5 years = 3,650 minutes = 60.83 hours)

Don't worry if you miss a day. Try not to, but if you do, no one will know and no one will care. Also, since it's only one line, it's easy to catch up the next day.

Make your one line a day journal part of your routine. Some people keep it by the side of their bed and enter a line before turning in.

What if I'm inspired to write more than one line?

Many people keep another journal for those times they want to capture more detail. Typically they don't write in those journals every day (or even every week or month). The extra journal is available for them when something inspires them to write in a longer format and the one line a day journal is the only constant.

Why don't I just do this online?

You can if you want to, but what people tell us is that they like the tangibility of a book like this. They like to hold it and feel the weight knowing that it represents moments of their life. They like flipping through it and seeing their own handwriting. They also like the privacy of not having their personal information readily available to people other than themselves (which is not guaranteed on line).

JANUARY

January 1

20 _____

20 _____

20 _____

20 _____

20 _____

January 2

20

20

20

20

20

January 3

20

20

20

20

20

January 4

20

20

20

20

20

January 5

20

20

20

20

20

January 6

20

20

20

20

20

January 7

20

20

20

20

20

January 8

20 _____

20 _____

20 _____

20 _____

20 _____

January 9

20___

20___

20___

20___

20___

January 10

20

20

20

20

20

January 11

20 _____

20 _____

20 _____

20 _____

20 _____

January 12

20 _____

20 _____

20 _____

20 _____

20 _____

January 13

20 _____

20 _____

20 _____

20 _____

20 _____

January 14

20

20

20

20

20

January 15

20

20

20

20

20

January 16

20

20

20

20

20

January 17

20 _____

20 _____

20 _____

20 _____

20 _____

January 18

20 _____

20 _____

20 _____

20 _____

20 _____

January 19

20

20

20

20

20

January 20

20

20

20

20

20

January 21

20

20

20

20

20

January 22

20

20

20

20

20

January 23

20

20

20

20

20

January 24

20

20

20

20

20

January 25

20

20

20

20

20

January 26

20

20

20

20

20

January 27

20 _____

20 _____

20 _____

20 _____

20 _____

January 28

20

20

20

20

20

January 29

20

20

20

20

20

January 30

20

20

20

20

20

January 31

20

20

20

20

20

FEBRUARY

February 1

20

20

20

20

20

February 2

20

20

20

20

20

February 3

20

20

20

20

20

February 4

20

20

20

20

20

February 5

20

20

20

20

20

February 6

20

20

20

20

20

February 7

20

20

20

20

20

February 8

20

20

20

20

20

February 9

20

20

20

20

20

February 10

20 _____

20 _____

20 _____

20 _____

20 _____

February 11

20 _____

20 _____

20 _____

20 _____

20 _____

February 12

20

20

20

20

20

February 13

20

20

20

20

20

February 14

20 _____

20 _____

20 _____

20 _____

20 _____

February 15

20

20

20

20

20

February 16

20

20

20

20

20

February 17

20

20

20

20

20

February 18

20

20

20

20

20

February 19

20 _____

20 _____

20 _____

20 _____

20 _____

February 20

20 _____

20 _____

20 _____

20 _____

20 _____

February 21

20 _____

20 _____

20 _____

20 _____

20 _____

February 22

20

20

20

20

20

February 23

20

20

20

20

20

February 24

20

20

20

20

20

February 25

20

20

20

20

20

February 26

20 _____

20 _____

20 _____

20 _____

20 _____

February 27

20

20

20

20

20

February 28

20

20

20

20

20

February 29 (Leap Year)

20

20

20

20

20

MARCH

March 1

20 _____

20 _____

20 _____

20 _____

20 _____

March 2

20

20

20

20

20

March 3

20

20

20

20

20

March 4

20

20

20

20

20

March 5

20

20

20

20

20

March 6

20

20

20

20

20

March 7

20

20

20

20

20

March 8

20 _____

20 _____

20 _____

20 _____

20 _____

March 9

20

20

20

20

20

March 10

20 _____

20 _____

20 _____

20 _____

20 _____

March 11

20 _____

20 _____

20 _____

20 _____

20 _____

March 12

20 _____

20 _____

20 _____

20 _____

20 _____

March 13

20

20

20

20

20

March 14

20

20

20

20

20

March 15

20

20

20

20

20

March 16

20

20

20

20

20

March 17

20 _____

20 _____

20 _____

20 _____

20 _____

March 18

20

20

20

20

20

March 19

20

20

20

20

20

March 20

20

20

20

20

20

March 21

20 _____

20 _____

20 _____

20 _____

20 _____

March 22

20 _____

20 _____

20 _____

20 _____

20 _____

March 23

20 _____

20 _____

20 _____

20 _____

20 _____

March 24

20

20

20

20

20

March 25

20

20

20

20

20

March 26

20 _____

20 _____

20 _____

20 _____

20 _____

March 27

20

20

20

20

20

March 28

20

20

20

20

20

March 29

20

20

20

20

20

March 30

20

20

20

20

20

March 31

20

20

20

20

20

APRIL

April 1

20

20

20

20

20

April 2

20

20

20

20

20

April 3

20

20

20

20

20

April 4

20

20

20

20

20

April 5

20

20

20

20

20

April 6

20

20

20

20

20

April 7

20 _____

20 _____

20 _____

20 _____

20 _____

April 8

20

20

20

20

20

April 9

20

20

20

20

20

April 10

20

20

20

20

20

April 11

20

20

20

20

20

April 12

20

20

20

20

20

April 13

20

20

20

20

20

April 14

20 _____

20 _____

20 _____

20 _____

20 _____

April 15

20

20

20

20

20

April 16

20

20

20

20

20

April 17

20

20

20

20

20

April 18

20

20

20

20

20

April 19

20

20

20

20

20

April 20

20

20

20

20

20

April 21

20 _____

20 _____

20 _____

20 _____

20 _____

April 22

20

20

20

20

20

April 23

20

20

20

20

20

April 24

20

20

20

20

20

April 25

20 _____

20 _____

20 _____

20 _____

20 _____

April 26

20

20

20

20

20

April 27

April 28

20

20

20

20

20

April 29

20

20

20

20

20

April 30

20

20

20

20

20

MAY

May 1

20

20

20

20

20

May 2

20

20

20

20

20

May 3

20

20

20

20

20

May 4

20

20

20

20

20

May 5

20

20

20

20

20

May 6

20

20

20

20

20

May 7

20

20

20

20

20

May 8

20 _____

20 _____

20 _____

20 _____

20 _____

May 9

20

20

20

20

20

May 10

20

20

20

20

20

May 11

20

20

20

20

20

May 12

20 _____

20 _____

20 _____

20 _____

20 _____

May 13

20

20

20

20

20

May 14

20 _____

20 _____

20 _____

20 _____

20 _____

May 15

20

20

20

20

20

May 16

20 _____

20 _____

20 _____

20 _____

20 _____

May 17

20

20

20

20

20

May 18

20

20

20

20

20

May 19

20

20

20

20

20

May 20

20

20

20

20

20

May 21

20

20

20

20

20

May 22

20 _____

20 _____

20 _____

20 _____

20 _____

May 23

20

20

20

20

20

May 24

20

20

20

20

20

May 25

20

20

20

20

20

May 26

20

20

20

20

20

May 27

20

20

20

20

20

May 27

20

20

20

20

20

May 28

20

20

20

20

20

May 29

20

20

20

20

20

May 30

May 31

20

20

20

20

20

JUNE

June 1

20

20

20

20

20

June 2

20

20

20

20

20

June 3

20 _____

20 _____

20 _____

20 _____

20 _____

June 4

20

20

20

20

20

June 5

20

20

20

20

20

June 6

20

20

20

20

20

June 7

20

20

20

20

20

June 8

20 _____

20 _____

20 _____

20 _____

20 _____

June 9

20

20

20

20

20

June 10

20 _____

20 _____

20 _____

20 _____

20 _____

June 11

20 _____

20 _____

20 _____

20 _____

20 _____

June 12

20

20

20

20

20

June 13

20

20

20

20

20

June 14

20

20

20

20

20

June 15

20

20

20

20

20

June 16

20

20

20

20

20

June 17

20 _____

20 _____

20 _____

20 _____

20 _____

June 18

20

20

20

20

20

June 19

20

20

20

20

20

June 20

20

20

20

20

20

June 21

20 _____

20 _____

20 _____

20 _____

20 _____

June 22

20

20

20

20

20

June 23

20

20

20

20

20

June 24

20

20

20

20

20

June 25

20

20

20

20

20

June 26

20

20

20

20

20

June 27

20

20

20

20

20

June 28

20 _____

_____

_____

_____

20 _____

_____

_____

_____

20 _____

_____

_____

_____

20 _____

_____

_____

_____

20 _____

_____

_____

_____

June 29

20

20

20

20

20

June 30

20 ___

20 ___

20 ___

20 ___

20 ___

JULY

July 1

20

20

20

20

20

July 2

20

20

20

20

20

July 3

20 _____

20 _____

20 _____

20 _____

20 _____

July 4

20

20

20

20

20

July 5

20

20

20

20

20

July 6

20

20

20

20

20

July 7

20

20

20

20

20

July 8

20

20

20

20

20

July 9

20

20

20

20

20

July 10

20

20

20

20

20

July 11

20

20

20

20

20

July 12

20

20

20

20

20

July 13

20

20

20

20

20

July 14

20 _____

20 _____

20 _____

20 _____

20 _____

July 15

20

20

20

20

20

July 16

20

20

20

20

20

July 17

20

20

20

20

20

July 18

20 _____

20 _____

20 _____

20 _____

20 _____

July 19

20 _____

20 _____

20 _____

20 _____

20 _____

July 20

20

20

20

20

20

July 21

20

20

20

20

20

July 22

20

20

20

20

20

July 23

20

20

20

20

20

July 24

20

20

20

20

20

July 25

20

20

20

20

20

July 26

20

20

20

20

20

July 27

20

20

20

20

20

July 28

20

20

20

20

20

July 29

20

20

20

20

20

July 30

20

20

20

20

20

July 31

20

20

20

20

20

AUGUST

August 1

20

20

20

20

20

August 2

20

20

20

20

20

August 3

20

20

20

20

20

August 4

20 _____

20 _____

20 _____

20 _____

20 _____

August 5

20 _____

20 _____

20 _____

20 _____

20 _____

August 6

20

20

20

20

20

August 7

20 _____

20 _____

20 _____

20 _____

20 _____

August 8

20 _____

20 _____

20 _____

20 _____

20 _____

August 9

20

20

20

20

20

August 10

20 _____

20 _____

20 _____

20 _____

20 _____

August 11

20

20

20

20

20

August 12

20

20

20

20

20

August 13

20 _____

20 _____

20 _____

20 _____

20 _____

August 14

20 ___

20 ___

20 ___

20 ___

20 ___

August 15

20

20

20

20

20

August 16

20

20

20

20

20

August 17

20

20

20

20

20

August 18

20

20

20

20

20

August 19

20

20

20

20

20

August 20

20

20

20

20

20

August 21

20 _____

20 _____

20 _____

20 _____

20 _____

August 22

20

20

20

20

20

August 23

20

20

20

20

20

August 24

20 _____

20 _____

20 _____

20 _____

20 _____

August 25

20

20

20

20

20

August 26

20 _____

20 _____

20 _____

20 _____

20 _____

August 27

20

20

20

20

20

August 28

20 _____

20 _____

20 _____

20 _____

20 _____

August 29

20 _____

20 _____

20 _____

20 _____

20 _____

August 30

20 _____

_____

_____

_____

20 _____

_____

_____

_____

20 _____

_____

_____

_____

20 _____

_____

_____

_____

20 _____

_____

_____

_____

August 31

20 _____

20 _____

20 _____

20 _____

20 _____

SEPTEMBER

September 1

20

20

20

20

20

September 2

20

20

20

20

20

September 3

20

20

20

20

20

September 4

20

20

20

20

20

September 5

20 _____

20 _____

20 _____

20 _____

20 _____

September 6

20

20

20

20

20

September 7

20 _____

20 _____

20 _____

20 _____

20 _____

September 8

20

20

20

20

20

September 9

20 _____

20 _____

20 _____

20 _____

20 _____

September 10

20

20

20

20

20

September 11

20

20

20

20

20

September 12

20

20

20

20

20

September 13

20

20

20

20

20

September 14

20 _____

20 _____

20 _____

20 _____

20 _____

September 15

20

20

20

20

20

September 16

20

20

20

20

20

September 17

20

20

20

20

20

September 18

20

20

20

20

20

September 19

20

20

20

20

20

September 20

20

20

20

20

20

September 21

20

20

20

20

20

September 22

20 _____

20 _____

20 _____

20 _____

20 _____

September 23

20

20

20

20

20

September 24

20

20

20

20

20

September 25

20

20

20

20

20

September 26

20 _____

20 _____

20 _____

20 _____

20 _____

September 27

20

20

20

20

20

September 28

20

20

20

20

20

September 29

20 _____

20 _____

20 _____

20 _____

20 _____

September 30

20

20

20

20

20

OCTOBER

October 1

20 _____

20 _____

20 _____

20 _____

20 _____

October 2

20

20

20

20

20

October 3

20

20

20

20

20

October 4

20_____

20_____

20_____

20_____

20_____

October 5

20

20

20

20

20

October 6

20

20

20

20

20

October 7

20

20

20

20

20

October 8

20

20

20

20

20

October 9

20

20

20

20

20

October 10

20

20

20

20

20

October 11

20

20

20

20

20

October 12

20 _____

20 _____

20 _____

20 _____

20 _____

October 13

20

20

20

20

20

October 14

20

20

20

20

20

October 15

20

20

20

20

20

October 16

20 _____

20 _____

20 _____

20 _____

20 _____

October 17

20

20

20

20

20

October 18

20 _____

20 _____

20 _____

20 _____

20 _____

October 19

20

20

20

20

20

October 20

20

20

20

20

20

October 21

20

20

20

20

20

October 22

20 _____

20 _____

20 _____

20 _____

20 _____

October 23

October 24

20 _____

20 _____

20 _____

20 _____

20 _____

October 25

20

20

20

20

20

October 26

20

20

20

20

20

October 27

20

20

20

20

20

October 28

20 _____

20 _____

20 _____

20 _____

20 _____

October 29

20

20

20

20

20

October 30

20

20

20

20

20

October 31

20

20

20

20

20

NOVEMBER

November 1

20 _____

20 _____

20 _____

20 _____

20 _____

November 2

20

20

20

20

20

November 3

20

20

20

20

20

November 4

20

20

20

20

20

November 5

20

20

20

20

20

November 6

20

20

20

20

20

November 7

20

20

20

20

20

November 8

20

20

20

20

20

November 9

20

20

20

20

20

November 10

20

20

20

20

20

November 11

20

20

20

20

20

November 12

20

20

20

20

20

November 13

20

20

20

20

20

November 14

20

20

20

20

20

November 15

20

20

20

20

20

November 16

20

20

20

20

20

November 17

20

20

20

20

20

November 18

20 _____

20 _____

20 _____

20 _____

20 _____

November 19

20

20

20

20

20

November 20

20

20

20

20

20

November 21

20

20

20

20

20

November 22

20

20

20

20

20

November 23

20

20

20

20

20

November 24

20

20

20

20

20

November 25

20

20

20

20

20

November 26

20

20

20

20

20

November 27

20

20

20

20

20

November 28

20

20

20

20

20

November 29

20

20

20

20

20

November 30

20

20

20

20

20

DECEMBER

December 1

20

20

20

20

20

December 2

20

20

20

20

20

December 3

20

20

20

20

20

December 4

20 _____

20 _____

20 _____

20 _____

20 _____

December 5

20

20

20

20

20

December 6

20

20

20

20

20

December 7

20

20

20

20

20

December 8

20

20

20

20

20

December 9

20

20

20

20

20

December 10

20

20

20

20

20

December 11

20

20

20

20

20

December 12

20 _____

20 _____

20 _____

20 _____

20 _____

December 13

20

20

20

20

20

December 14

20

20

20

20

20

December 15

20

20

20

20

20

December 16

20 _____

20 _____

20 _____

20 _____

20 _____

December 17

20

20

20

20

20

December 18

20 _____

20 _____

20 _____

20 _____

20 _____

December 19

20

20

20

20

20

December 20

20 _____

20 _____

20 _____

20 _____

20 _____

December 21

20

20

20

20

20

December 22

20

20

20

20

20

December 23

20

20

20

20

20

December 24

20 _____

20 _____

20 _____

20 _____

20 _____

December 25

20

20

20

20

20

December 26

20

20

20

20

20

December 27

20

20

20

20

20

December 28

20

20

20

20

20

December 29

20

20

20

20

20

December 30

20

20

20

20

20

December 31

20

20

20

20

20

A Great Gift Idea: Give a friend or family member a 5-Year One Line a Day Journal (available from amazon.com and other retailers)

To Compliment Your Journaling: You can achieve greater levels of success with one or both of these personal growth manuals from the *Think · Act · Succeed* series available from amazon.com and other retailers: